The Unofficial Breaking Bad Cookbook

Food with Many Shades

By - Rene Reed

License Notes

Table of Contents

Introduction

The inspiration behind this cookbook came to us right from the opening scene of the first season of the show. We watched Skyler cooking eggs for Walt's birthday breakfast and could never recover from the power of the scene. There are many similar food moments that kept probing us to go for this special cookbook to entertain the Breaking Bad fans in a different and delicious way.

This cookbook has a unique color scheme, creative graphics and the recipes included in it are the cherries on the top. Our culinary experts have put very much effort into creating and recreating these recipes and turning them into the easiest possible methods while maintaining their authentic taste. Give these yummy recipes a try and you will become a fan of these oh-so-different recipes!

Starters, Snacks, and Drinks

Carrot soup

Walter and Skyler White had a humble lifestyle as Walter was a school teacher in this blockbuster series. This carrot soup reminds us of their simple but happy, fun-filled, and content life. We have tweaked the common recipe of this soup for better taste. Moreover, this soup is a perfect pick for the most drool-worthy appetizer in your formal parties.

Serving size: 6

Cooking time: 1 hour 20 minutes

Ingredients:

- Chopped carrots 3 lb.
- Chopped garlic cloves 3
- Chicken stock 6 cups
- Salt 1 ½ teaspoons
- Butter ¼ lb.
- Dried dill weed 2 tablespoons

Instructions:

Combine the butter, salt, dill weed, garlic, carrots, and chicken stock on high heat in a stockpot.

Bring it to boiling and decrease the heat. Simmer for about half an hour and until carrots become tender.

Puree this soup in a blender then return it back to the stockpot.

Simmer for 45 minutes more.

Season with some extra garlic or dill if desired.

Chamomile tea

The Whites in Breaking Bad went through a hell of problems and we thought that they really needed some soothing, calming concoction to relax. This chamomile tea is a natural soothing agent which helps you get rid of that unnecessary stress you are going through. Whip up this aromatic tea to have a relaxing moment right in the middle of the hectic day or to enjoy a lazy weekend in peace.

Serving size: 2

Cooking time: 7 minutes

Ingredients:

- Dried Chamomile 3 teaspoons
- Water 2 cups
- Honey to taste

Instructions:

In a saucepan, heat the water on high.

When water starts to boil, turn off the heat.

Add dried chamomile and keep the tea covered for one minute.

Strain the tea into the cups and add honey, swirl it and serve.

Blue Raspberry Pineapple Slush

Blue is the special color we give to the food inspired from Breaking Bad. If you intend to throw a party with Breaking Bad as the theme, this drink is a perfect option for you. The recipe is easy, and the flavor and look of this special drink are sophisticated to be a part of your formal, fancy parties, and gatherings.

Serving size: 6

Cooking time: 5 minutes

Ingredients:

- Pineapple juice 3 cups
- "Blue raspberry" syrup 1 cup
- Water 1 cup
- Lemon juice 1 cup
- Ginger ale 2 cans
- Sugar 1/2 cup

Instructions:

Combine all the ingredients except ginger ale in a container safe from the freezer.

Freeze the mixture until solid.

Remove from the freezer one hour before serving and let it thaw.

Start breaking up the mixture using a fork and combine it with the ginger ale while stirring until the mixture is pourable and slushy.

Lemonade

To cope with the hot Mexican summers, the Whites must need some super refreshing drink. This lemonade recipe is loaded with vitamin C and quenches you on the hottest summer days. The pleasant tangy aroma of lemon is enough to wake up all your dull and down senses and raise your energy level.

Serving size: 10

Cooking time: 15 minutes

Ingredients:

- White sugar 3 cups
- Thinly sliced lemons 12
- Ice cubes 4 trays
- Cold water 8 cups

Instructions:

Slice the lemons crosswise. Remove the seeds.

Add the lemon slices to the punch bowl.

Put the sugar on top of lemons and pound them along with the sugar using a spoon.

Keep stirring until the sugar gets dissolved.

Add the ice cubes. Stir in the cold water, then serve the lemon drink in big glasses.

Special Purple Fruit Salad with Honey and Lavender Syrup

The special foods that cancer patients are asked to consume are the fruits and fruits that are darker in color because they are packed with the antioxidants to boost immunity. Here goes the recipe of a special purple salad which is not only healthy but proves to be the real treat for your taste buds. Figs, plums, and berries give you a punch of taste you have never tasted before, while lavender creates the signature aroma for this yummy treat.

Serving size: 5

Cooking time: 10 minutes

Ingredients:

- Dried lavender 1 tablespoon
- Water 1/2 cup
- Purple fruit 8 cups (grapes, blueberries, plums, figs)
- Honey 1/4 cup
- Lemon juice of 1 lemon

Instructions:

Combine water and honey in a saucepan and bring to simmering on low heat.

Add the lavender. Simmer for 10 minutes and until thick and reduced while stirring occasionally.

Remove from the heat. Allow it to cool. Steep for 30 minutes.

Wash the fruit and cut.

Combine the fruit with lemon juice and drizzle lavender syrup on it to taste.

Chicken cordon bleu

After having earned that crazy money, Walter White could afford a luxury lifestyle and food was no exception. This recipe is an elite option and suits the best when you want to enjoy a special dinner with your family on special occasions. Moreover, it makes a perfect starter for your formal gatherings too.

Serving size: 4

Cooking time: 55 minutes

Ingredients:

- Softened butter 2 tablespoons
- Fully cooked ham 4 thin slices
- Swiss cheese 4 thin slices
- Dried thyme 1 teaspoon
- Chicken breast halves boneless and skinless 4 of ½ lb. each
- All-purpose flour 1/2 cup
- Dried oregano 1 teaspoon
- Bacon strips 8
- Dry bread crumbs ¾ cup
- Large eggs 2
- Garlic powder 1/2 teaspoon
- 2% milk 1/2 cup
- Shredded Parmesan cheese ¼ cup

Instructions:

Flatten the chicken breasts to make them 1/8 inch thick and spread butter inside.

Sprinkle the chicken with thyme and top with one cheese and ham slice and roll it up.

Wrap each chicken piece with bacon (2 slices) then secure them with the toothpicks.

Beat milk and eggs in a bowl and place flour in a different bowl.

Combine the cheese, oregano, garlic powder, and bread crumbs. Dip each breast piece into the mixture of egg then flour for coating. Dip again into the mixture of the egg. Coat with the crumbs.

Place the chicken on the greased baking sheet and bake it for 45 minutes at 350 F uncovered and until the juices become clear.

Deep-fried guacamole

This recipe is one of our most favorite among this entire collection for many reasons. It has that authentic Mexican origin, it is a healthier fried item and yes, we can serve it at our most formal parties and dinners. You are welcome to enjoy it as a snack too. Although our creative chefs have perfected the recipe, yet you are free to make any amendments according to your own taste preferences.

Serving size: 4

Cooking time: 30 minutes

Ingredients:

- Minced red onion 1 tablespoon
- Pitted and peeled avocadoes 2
- Minced cilantro 1 tablespoon
- All-purpose flour ¾ cup
- Baking powder a pinch
- Minced and seeded jalapeño 1 tablespoon
- Corn flour ½ cup
- Lime juice of 1 lime
- Seltzer 12 ounces
- Salt to taste
- Vegetable oil to fry

Instructions:

Mash avocado until it's smooth.

Dice another avocado and mix them together.

Add salt, lime juice, cilantro, onion, and jalapeño. Make 14 oval patties from the mixture and place them on the baking sheet lined with foil. Freeze for an hour.

Place flour ¼ cup in a bowl. Dust the frozen patties lightly.

In a different bowl, mix the rest of the flour, salt a teaspoon, baking powder, and cornflour. Stir in the seltzer.

Heat the oil in a skillet and coat the floured patties in the batter. Fry for 3 minutes and until golden brown on medium heat. Turn them to fry from the other side.

Drain on the paper towel and serve.

Nachos supreme

If you are looking for a perfect Mexican starter that tells the tale of its origin without having you introducing it, this recipe ends your quest. Loaded with traditional Mexican flavors and spices, this recipe would create floods in everyone's mouths. You are welcome to adjust the spices and seasoning but we recommend going for our recipe as our culinary experts have perfected it almost perfectly.

Serving size: 2

Cooking time: 25 minutes

Ingredients:

- Undiluted tomato soup condensed 2/3 cup
- Uncooked instant rice 3/4 cup
- Lean ground beef ½ lb.
- Taco seasoning 2 tablespoons
- Water 3/4 cup
- Tortilla chips as you like
- Optional toppings (sour cream, salsa, cheddar cheese shredded, and shredded lettuce)

Instructions:

Cook the beef in a skillet until it is not pink any longer on medium heat and drain.

Stir on the taco seasoning, soup, and water and bring to boiling. Stir in the rice and cover.

Remove from heat and let them stand for 5 minutes and until the rice becomes tender.

Spoon it onto the serving plates and top with the optional toppings if desired.

Serve with the tortilla chips and enjoy.

Breakfasts

Eggs and bacon

Yes, we know that it is a very common breakfast recipe and probably everyone knows how to make eggs and bacon. But how could we miss out on the opening of this mind-blowing thriller where Skyler and Walter enjoy eggs and bacon for breakfast for Walter's 50th birthday. Let's relive that favorite memory of all of us with this oh-so-homely breakfast.

Serving size: 1

Cooking time: 10 minutes

Ingredients:

- Eggs 2
- Sliced bacon 0.14 lb.
- Fresh thyme (optional)
- Cherry tomatoes (optional)

Instructions:

On medium heat, fry the bacon in a pan until it becomes crispy. Put it aside on the plate.

In the same pan, half fry the eggs in the grease of bacon.

Cook the eggs as you like.

Slice the cheery tomato in half pieces—Fry at a similar time.

Sprinkle the pepper and salt to taste and enjoy.

Eggs and chorizo wraps

Let us wrap those oh-so-common eggs into some fancy chorizos for a yummy breakfast. This recipe is an ideal choice for breaking the monotony of the cereals, porridge, and pancake breakfast you have every day. Start your day with a yummy twist while savoring every bite of these eggs and chorizo wraps. Our recommendation is to add that optional topping for an added dose of flavor and texture!

Serving size: 6

Cooking time: 20 minutes

Ingredients:

- Fresh chorizo ¾ lb.
- 2% milk 2 tablespoons
- Shredded cheddar cheese 1 cup
- Large eggs 6
- Warmed flour tortillas 6 of 8 inches
- Optional toppings (salsa, minced fresh cilantro, green onions, thinly sliced)

Instructions:

Remove the chorizo from the casings.

Cook the chorizo on medium heat in a skillet for 7 to 8 minutes while breaking it into crumbles. Drain then return to the pan.

Whisk milk and eggs in a bowl until blended well. Add the mixture of egg to the chorizo.

Cook while stirring to thicken the eggs. Then stir in the cheese and spoon egg mixture (1/2 cup) in the middle of every tortilla.

Add the toppings of liking and fold the sides and bottom of the tortilla over the filling and roll it up.

Beef enchiladas

Breakfast is not always a quick fix of a cereal bowl or a toast with jam and butter. Our cooking experts are introducing you to a whole new world of breakfast delicacies and this recipe is on the top of the list. Make this filling, wholesome, and lip-smacking breakfast this weekend and surprise your loved ones with your culinary skills.

Serving size: 28

Cooking time: 50 minutes

Ingredients:

- Chopped medium onions 4
- Divided enchilada sauce 4 cans of 0.6 lb.
- Undrained chili beans 4 cans of 1 lb.
- Shredded cheddar cheese 4 cups
- Divided salsa 1 jar of 1 lb.
- Ground beef 4 lb.
- Flour tortillas 28 of 8 inches
- Drained, sliced ripe olives 2 cans
- Canola oil as needed

Instructions:

Cook the onions and beef in the stockpot on medium heat and until the meat is not pink any longer and drain.

Stir in half enchilada sauce, salsa 1 cup, and beans and set aside.

Heat oil ¼ inch in a skillet and dip every tortilla for 3 seconds in hot oil from each side and drain on the paper towels.

Top every tortilla with beef mixture 2/3 cup and roll-up. Place them on baking dishes with the seam side facing down.

Drizzle with the rest of the salsa and enchilada sauce. Sprinkle with olives and cheese.

Bake uncovered for about 20 to 25 minutes at 350 F and until bubbly.

Granola

Teaching is a tough job and mornings are specially packed for the teachers; it must be with our protagonist, Walter White, in Breaking Bad. Later on, while earning that bad money, we are sure he would have rare chances to have a peaceful, sit-down breakfast. This recipe is a quick fix for all those Breaking Bad fans who are always in a rush and have limited time for breakfast. Make a big batch of this granola and enjoy it as an on-the-go breakfast!

Serving size: 12

Cooking time: 30 minutes

Ingredients

- Flaked coconut 1 cup
- Cinnamon ¾ teaspoon
- Slivered toasted almonds 1 cup
- Almond oil ¼ cup
- Rolled oats 2 ½ cups
- Honey ½ cup

Instructions:

Combine the oats, toasted almonds, cinnamon, and coconut together.

Blend in the honey with the oil. Drizzle it over the mixture of almond and oats. Toss well to mix.

Bake in the oven at about 350 F for half an hour while occasionally stirring.

Remove from the oven and loosen it with the spatula. Cool it down and enjoy.

Mexican breakfast cups

This bombastic recipe is loaded with flavorful traditional Mexican ingredients and you get a blast of cheese in every bite. These breakfast cups are far beyond your hash brown, omelet, and all the other typical breakfasts you enjoy in routine. Our experts have tweaked the original recipe to make it a perfect fit for everyone's taste and we are sure you would adore it!

Serving size: 6

Cooking time: 35 minutes

Ingredients

- Frozen hash brown potatoes shredded 1 cup
- Mexican cheese blend shredded ¼ cup
- Turkey bacon strips 18 (cut in half)
- Pepper and salt a dash
- 2% milk 2 teaspoons
- Chopped fresh parsley and green onion
- Butter 2 teaspoons
- Eggs 2

Instructions:

Preheat the oven to about 375 F.

Line mini-muffin pan with 12 cups and with the bacon pieces and crisscross strips to resemble a wheel spoke.

Crumple twelve strips of the aluminum foil of 3 inches and place them in the cups so that the bacon does not slide.

Bake for 15 to 20 minutes and until the bacon becomes crisp.

Cook the potatoes as per instructions and whisk pepper, salt, milk, and eggs in a bowl.

Heat butter in a skillet on medium heat and pour in the mixture of egg and cook while stirring until the eggs become thick and done.

Transfer the bacon cups to the baking sheet and remove the foil. Spoon the scrambled eggs and hash brown into the cups and sprinkle the cheese.

Broil it for 3 to 5 minutes 3-4 inches from heat and until the cheese melts. Sprinkle with parsley and green onion and voila!

Crème brulee French Toast

This recipe belongs to the times when our protagonists had become filthy rich and could relish elite stuff. This recipe takes the French toast game up to the level you never thought of before. The creamy texture and that caramelized sugar's smell drive your senses crazy with the first bite. Make it to treat your taste buds the luxurious way they deserve to be treated.

Serving size: 4

Cooking time: 1 hour 5 minutes

Ingredients:

- 2% milk 1 cup
- French bread 6 slices
- Ground cinnamon 1/2 teaspoon
- Vanilla extract 1 teaspoon
- Large eggs 4
- Half-and-half cream 1 cup
- Sugar 2 tablespoons
- Confectioners' sugar (optional)
- Crushed cornflakes, 1 cup (optional)
- Maple syrup as you like

Instructions:

Place the bread slices on the ungreased dish.

Whisk the cinnamon, half-and-half vanilla, sugar, milk, and eggs in a bowl and pour it over the bread.

Soak the bread for 2 minutes and coat it with crumbs of cornflake from all sides.

Place the bread in the greased baking pan and freeze for 45 minutes or until firm.

Transfer the toast to the airtight container in a freezer.

When you want to use these slices, place them on the greased sheet for baking and bake for about 8 minutes at 425 F.

Turn the slices and bake for 10 more minutes and until golden in color.

Sprinkle the confectioners' sugar if you like and serve it with the maple syrup.

Chilaquiles

Add some color, fun, and flavor with the crunchy texture to your morning with this Mexican breakfast recipe. This easy-to-make recipe is all you need to take a break from oh-so-boring sweet breakfasts you have been gulping down for ages. The crunchy veggies and crispy tortilla chips, along with chorizos, make it a drool-worthy treat for you!

Serving size: 4

Cooking time: 30 minutes

Ingredients:

- Finely chopped medium onion 1
- Tortilla chips 4 cups
- Fresh chorizo ½ lb.
- Lean ground beef ½ lb.
- Undrained green chiles and diced tomatoes 1 can
- Fresh cilantro chopped
- Undrained diced tomatoes and mild green chiles 1 can
- Minced garlic clove 1
- Monterey jack cheese shredded 1 cup
- Optional toppings: sliced red onion, diced avocado, and sour cream

Instructions:

Preheat an oven to about 350 F.

Cook chorizo and beef with garlic and onion on medium heat in a skillet for 5 to 7 minutes and until not pink any longer. Stir in the tomatoes and bring them to boiling.

Layer chips 2 cups in a greased 8-inch baking dish along with cheese ½ cup, and meat mixture half and repeat the layers.

Bake for 12 to 15 minutes uncovered and until the cheese melts.

Sprinkle with the cilantro and serve with the toppings if desired.

Mexican breakfast tacos

Tacos are not only for snacking and starters but we turned them into this super-tasty breakfast option for all the Breaking Bad fans. Once again, taking the inspiration from the setting of this super hit thriller, our chefs selected this recipe for you to have some yummy twist in your menu.

Serving size: 4

Cooking time: 10 minutes

Ingredients:

- Sweet pickle relish 2 tablespoons
- Tilapia fillets 4
- Divided kosher salt 0.63 teaspoon
- Ground red pepper ½ teaspoon
- Chili powder 1 teaspoon
- Corn tortillas 8
- Cilantro leaves ½ cup
- Lime cut into wedges 1
- Ripe avocado cut into wedges 1
- Ground cumin ½ teaspoon
- Medium tomato cut into wedges 1
- Canola mayonnaise 3 tablespoons
- Freshly ground black pepper ½ teaspoon

Instructions:

On medium heat, heat the grill pan. Coat the pan with cooking spray.

Sprinkle the fish with the cumin, red pepper, black pepper, salt, and chili powder evenly.

Add the fish to the pan. Cook for 3 minutes from every side, and until the fish becomes flaked easily. Cut the fillet into small slices.

Combine the black pepper, salt, pickle relish, and mayonnaise in a bowl. Heat the tortillas as per package instructions.

Divide the tomato, avocado, and fish evenly among the tortillas.

Drizzle the tacos on the mayonnaise mixture.

Sprinkle the cilantro on it. Serve with lime wedges.

Main Course

Mushroom and chicken pizza

We have been watching pizza coming in front of our eyes for so many times while watching Breaking Bad. Do you remember the pizza that accidentally reaches the rooftop by Walter while having a row with Skyler in season three? Let's relive that funny memory with this mouthwatering mushroom and chicken pizza. We suggest you to savor this pizza while binge-watching breaking Bad for an extra dose of fun!

Serving size: 4

Cooking time: 20 minutes

Ingredients:

- Fresh mushrooms sliced 1 cup
- Mini pizza crusts prebaked 4
- Melted butter 2 tablespoons
- Shredded cheddar cheese 1 cup
- Salad dressing ranch or blue cheese 1 cup
- Cooked chicken shredded or cubed 2 cups
- Hot pepper sauce ¼ cup
- Mozzarella cheese shredded 1 cup

Instructions:

Place the crusts in an ungreased baking pan of 15x10x1 inches.

Combine the pepper sauce, butter, mushrooms, and chicken in a bowl.

Spread the salad dressing on the crusts and top it with the mixture of chicken and mushroom. Sprinkle it with cheeses.

Bake the pizza for about 10 to 15 minutes and until the edges become light brown at 425 F.

Let the pizza stand for about 5 minutes then serve.

Fried chicken

Los Pollos Hermanos was the famous restaurant in Breaking Bad where was the hub of all the drug deals in the southwest. However, for the foodies like us and the other breaking Bad fans, this restaurant was famous for its fried chicken and we just lived the way that sizzling, appetizing fried chicken used to look in the movie. Let's recreate that restaurant by preparing this delicious fried chicken with our recipe. The crunch with every munch will make you try it again and again!

Serving size: 4

Cooking time: 35 minutes

Ingredients:

- All-purpose flour 1 ¾ cups
- Dried thyme 1 tablespoon
- Paprika 1 tablespoon
- Salt 2 teaspoons
- Garlic powder 2 teaspoons
- Pepper 1 teaspoon
- Large egg 1
- 2% milk 1/3 cup
- Lemon juice 2 tablespoons
- fryer chicken cut up 1 (3 to 4 lb.)
- Oil to deep-fry

Instructions:

Mix the first six ingredients in a bowl.

Whisk the lemon juice, milk, and egg in a different bowl until blended.

Dip the chicken in the mixture of flour to coat and shake off the excess.

Dip in the mixture of egg then in the flour mixture.

Deep fry the chicken for about 6 to 10 minutes from each side at 375 F and until the skin becomes golden brown.

Drain the chicken on the paper towels and enjoy.

Bourbon Pecan Chicken

This oh-so-different recipe is a luxurious combination of chicken, bourbon, and pecan. The best part after its novelty is its cooking time which is far lesser than most of the main course dishes. Our talented team has amazingly recreated the recipe which fits in everybody's taste and anybody with basic cooking skills can make it easily. You can serve it with any side dish of your choice or on its own. Give it a try to have a new favorite main course dish.

Serving size: 8

Cooking time: 30 minutes

Ingredients:

- Finely chopped pecans ½ cup
- Dry bread crumbs ½ cup
- Chicken breast halves skinless and boneless 8
- Melted clarified butter ¼ cup
- Dijon mustard ¼ cup
- Bourbon whiskey 2 ⅔ tablespoons
- Dark brown sugar ¼ cup
- Soy sauce 2 tablespoons
- Worcestershire sauce 1 teaspoon
- Unsalted butter (cut into cubes) ¾ cup
- Sliced green onions ½ cup

Instructions:

Stir together butter 2 tbsp, bread crumbs, and pecans. Spread this mixture on the plate and press the chicken in the mixture for coating from both sides.

Heat the rest of the butter in a skillet on medium heat.

Place the chicken breasts coated in this pan and fry from both sides for 10 minutes each side and until browned nicely and chicken is done.

Whisk the Worcestershire sauce, soy sauce, bourbon, brown sugar, and Dijon mustard in a saucepan until smooth.

Bring to simmering on medium heat and remove from the heat. Whisk unsalted butter ¾ cup in it.

Arrange the breasts of the chicken on a serving plate and pour the sauce on the chicken. Sprinkle with the green onions.

Sliders with Blue Cheese and Pickled Onions

This slider burger represents the fast food we watched people eating during our favorite show, Breaking Bad. This easy-to-make recipe makes a favorite dinner or lunch if you have kids or teenagers around. However, the adults equally savor this super tasty recipe. Try it and you will forget those fancy burger joints.

Serving size: 4

Cooking time: 2 hours 18 minutes

Ingredients:

- Lukewarm water 3/4 cup
- Butter 2 tablespoons
- Flour 3 ½ cups
- Salt 1 1/4 teaspoons
- Eggs 2 (reserve 1 egg white)
- Instant yeast 1 tablespoon
- Sugar 1/4 cup
- Sesame seeds as needed
- Melted butter optional

For Pickled Onions

- Red onions 2
- Sugar 2 tablespoons
- Cider or white vinegar 1 to 2 cups
- Salt 2 teaspoons

For Assembly

- Fresh slider buns
- Blue cheese
- Broiled or grilled beef patties
- Pickled onions
- Greens optional
- Mayo as needed

Instructions:

Combine yeast, salt, sugar, flour, egg yolk 1, egg 1, and water in a food processor and blend well until soft.

Cover this dough. Let it rise for 1 hour and until doubled.

Punch down the dough gently and divide it for around 20 slider-sized buns.

Roll every dough piece into a ball. Place it on a lightly greased baking sheet.

Flatten it gently and cover it with a towel. Let it rise for an hour.

Preheat an oven to about 375 F.

Whisk the reserved white of the egg with water 2 tbsp. Brush it gently on bun tops. Sprinkle with the sesame seeds.

Bake these buns for 12 to 15 minutes and until golden.

Brush with melted butter if you like.

Slice the onions into rings and bring a pot filled with water to boil.

Drop the onions in it for a minute then drain and cool slightly.

Transfer it to the container having a lid and cover it with the vinegar. Add sugar and salt 2 tsp.

Stir and allow to sit for one hour, then use.

Assemble everything in the buns and enjoy.

Rosemary braised lamb shank

This super-elite dish is going to be the glory of your formal, multicourse meals and we are sure about it. The aroma of rosemary, the melting in the mouth texture, and the perfect blend of ingredients make it a perfect pick for everyone, even those who are not very confident about their cooking skills. Try this recipe from our chefs and you are all set to amaze the people with your culinary expertise.

Serving size: 8

Cooking time: 6 hours 25 minutes

Ingredients:

- Pepper 3/4 teaspoon
- Salt 1 teaspoon
- Butter 1 tablespoon
- Lamb shanks 4 (1.25 lb. each)
- White wine 1/2 cup
- Peeled and cut into chunks of 1-inch medium parsnips 3
- Peeled and cut into chunks of 1-inch large carrots 2
- Peeled and cut into chunks of 1-inch medium turnips 2
- Chopped large tomatoes 2
- Chopped large onion 1
- Minced garlic cloves 4
- Beef broth 2 cups
- Thawed frozen peas 1 package of 0.6 lb. each
- Chopped fresh parsley 1/3 cup
- Minced fresh rosemary 2 tablespoons

Instructions:

Rub the pepper and salt over the lamb.

Heat the butter on medium heat in a skillet and brown the meat.

Transfer the meat to a slow cooker and add wine to the skillet. Stir wine for a minute to loosen the brown bits.

Pour the mixture over the lamb and add the broth, garlic, onion, tomatoes, turnips, carrots, and parsnips. Cook covered for 6 to 8 hours on low until the meat becomes tender.

Remove the lamb and keep it warm. Stir in rosemary, parsley, and peas and heat it through.

Serve the lamb with the vegetables.

Chilean Fish Stew Recipe

Gustav Fring is an important character in breaking Bad with a huge fan following. This recipe takes inspiration from his native land and its famous cuisine, the Chilean. This fish stew tastes heavenly, far beyond the lamb and chicken stew. The hit spices and other special ingredients make it a drool-worthy treat for your taste buds. We are sure you will prize it as your favorite recipe after giving it a try.

Serving size: 4

Cooking time: 20 minutes

Ingredients:

- Peeled and deveined large shrimp ½ lb
- Chopped onion 2 cups
- Celery ¼ inch thick slices 1 cup
- Minced garlic cloves 3
- Carrot slices ¼ inch thick 1 cup
- Sliced jalapeño pepper 1
- Halibut (bite-size pieces) 1 lb
- Dry white wine 1 cup
- Olive oil 1 tablespoon
- Lime wedges
- Cubed and peeled red potato or Yukon gold 2 cups
- Chopped fresh cilantro ½ cup
- Chicken broth 4 cups
- Undrained crushed tomatoes 1 can
- Cilantro sprigs (optional)

Instructions:

Heat the oil in a Dutch oven on medium heat.

Add jalapeño, garlic, celery, carrot, and onion in a pan. Sauté for 5 minutes and until tender.

Stir in the tomatoes, cilantro, wine, potato, and broth. Bring them to boiling.

Reduce heat. Simmer for about 15 minutes and until the potato becomes tender.

Add shrimp and fish and cook for 5 more minutes and until they are done.

Ladle stew into 4 bowls and serve it with the lime wedges.

Garnish the stew with cilantro if desired.

Cajun seafood pasta

This oh-so-fancy dish is all you need to offer to your special guests on very special occasions. This recipe is the yummiest combo of Italian ingredients, seafood, and our local cuisine. We understand that cooking seafood is not everyone's cup of tea and our highly talented cooking experts have provided you with step-by-step guidance. You get to know everything right, from the measurements of the ingredients to the method for a perfect serving of this Cajun seafood pasta.

Serving size: 6

Cooking time: 10 minutes

Ingredients:

- Heavy whipping cream 2 cups
- Chopped fresh basil 1 tablespoon
- Salt 2 teaspoons
- Chopped fresh thyme 1 tablespoon
- Ground black pepper 2 teaspoons
- Crushed red pepper flakes 1 ½ teaspoons
- Ground white pepper 1 teaspoon
- Chopped green onions 1 cup
- Chopped parsley 1 cup
- Peeled, deveined shrimp 1 ½ lb.
- Scallops 1 ½ lb.
- Shredded Swiss cheese ½ cup
- Dry fettuccine pasta 1 lb.
- Grated parmesan cheese ½ cup

Instructions:

Cook the pasta in salted boiling water until it is al dente.

Pour the cream into a skillet and cook on medium heat while stirring until starts boiling.

Reduce the heat and add parsley, onions, peppers, salt, and herbs. Simmer for 8 minutes and until thickened.

Stir in the seafood and cook until the shrimp is not transparent any longer. Stir in the cheeses and blend well.

Drain the pasta and serve the sauce over the noodles.

Crab stuffed lobster tail

While dealing with the drug dealers, the dinner tables were super-luxury and, of course, highly tempting for the people like us. This recipe is superbly high-end we are sure that if you are a true fan of Breaking Bad, you must have developed a love for seafood also.

Serving size: 2

Cooking time: 25 minutes

Ingredients:

- Lump blue crab meat ½ lb.
- Finely minced parsley 1/2 teaspoon
- Mayonnaise 1/4 cup
- Lemon juice 1/2 teaspoon
- Worcestershire sauce 1/2 teaspoon
- Bread crumbs 1 tablespoon
- Egg white 1
- Sea salt or old bay seasoning 1/4 teaspoon
- Lobster tails medium 2
- Butter melted 2 teaspoons
- Lemon wedges 2

Instructions:

Preheat the oven to about 425 F.

Whisk the Old Bay seasoning and mayonnaise in a medium bowl and gently toss the crab into this mixture but do not break the crab pieces.

Pulp the lobster shells edges and lift the meat of the tail gently to rest it on the shells.

Place the lobster tails on the baking sheet and brush its tops with the melted butter.

Divide evenly and press the crab mixture gently into the tops.

Bake for 10 to 12 minutes and until the tails become opaque and the crab is browned. Then serve with the lemon wedges.

Taco lasagna

Italy and Mexico both combine well for this fusion of pasta and tacos recipe. Feel the flavors of the Italian mafia leaders and the Mexican drug lords in this super tasty, exclusive recipe. Most of the ingredients like red beans, cheese, and tacos are Mexican but the Italian lasagna remains dominant. Try it for a different lasagna flavor than those chicken, vegetable, and cheese pasta.

Serving size: 9

Cooking time: 45 minutes

Ingredients:

- Ground beef 1 lb.
- Chopped green pepper 1/2 cup
- Water 2/3 cup
- Chopped onion 1/2 cup
- Taco seasoning 1 envelope
- Rinsed and drained black beans 1 can of 0.9 lb.
- Undrained mexican diced tomatoes 1 can of 0.9 lb.
- Flour tortillas 6 of 8 inches
- Refried beans 1 can of 1 lb.
- Mexican cheese blend shredded 3 cups

Instructions:

Cook the onion, green pepper, and beef in a skillet on medium heat until the meat is not pink any longer and drain.

Add taco seasoning and water and bring to boiling. Reduce the heat and simmer for about 2 minutes uncovered.

Stir in tomatoes and black beans. Simmer it for about 10 minutes uncovered.

Place tortillas (two) in the greased baking dish of 13x9-in. Spread it with half beef mixture and half refried beans and sprinkle 1 cup of cheese on it. Repeat these layers and top with the rest of the cheese and tortillas.

Cover it and bake for 25 to 30 minutes at 350 F and until it's heated through and the cheese melts.

Desserts

Carrot cake

This very common cake recipe is from those good old days of the Whites from the Breaking Bad. Let's cherish those good memories with this recipe which our culinary experts have developed so lovingly. You might come across many recipes of carrot cake over the internet but this one is going to be your new favorite and we bet on that!

Serving size: 24

Cooking time: 1 hour

Ingredients:

- Grated carrots 4 cups
- Chopped walnuts ¾ cup
- All-purpose flour 2 cups
- Baking soda 2 teaspoons
- White sugar 2 cups
- Baking powder 2 teaspoons
- Vegetable oil 1 ⅓ cups
- Ground cinnamon 2 teaspoons
- Salt ½ teaspoon
- Eggs 4

Instructions:

Preheat the oven to about 350 F.

Grease a pan of 9x13 inches.

Sift the cinnamon, salt, baking soda, baking powder, and flour and set them aside.

Mix the eggs and sugar in a bowl until pale and thick.

Stir the oil in it and mix the dry ingredients gradually.

Fold the nuts and carrots in it. Spread the mixture evenly in the pan.

Bake for about 45 minutes in the oven.

Cool it down and frost with cream cheese frosting of your liking and there you go!

Creamy caramel flan

This Mexican will be the real showstopper in your next multicourse meal or any feast. The caramel and cream combine for a last of taste and texture. Every bite of this scrumptious dessert melts in your mouth and you forget to watch your calorie intake.

Serving size: 10

Cooking time: 1 hour 15 minutes

Ingredients:

- Sugar 3/4 cup
- Water 1/4 cup
- Softened cream cheese 1 package of ½ lb.
- Large eggs 5
- Sweetened condensed milk 1 can of 0.9 lb.
- Evaporated milk 1 can of ¾ lb.
- Vanilla extract 1 teaspoon

Instructions:

Cook water and sugar on medium heat in a saucepan until golden and melted in 15 minutes.

Brush down the crystals with extra water if needed on the pan's side.

Quickly pour it into the ungreased soufflé dish and tilt it for coating the bottom and let it stand for about 10 minutes.

Preheat the oven to about 350 F.

Beat cream cheese in a bowl until smooth. Beat in the eggs until combined. Then, add the rest of the ingredients and mix well.

Pour the caramelized sugar and place the dish in the larger baking pan.

Pour the boiling water in the pan to about 1 inch and bake for 50 to 60 minutes and until the middle is set.

Remove the dish and place it on a wire rack to cool for an hour. Then refrigerate overnight.

Run the knife around the edges to unmold and invert on a big serving platter. Spoon the sauce over every serving and enjoy.

Skyler White Cupcakes with Dulce de Leche and Marshmallow Frosting

Taking Skyler White's name as the symbol and inspiration, this recipe of cupcakes is one of our favorite as the hard-core fans of the Breaking Bad series. The added flavor and texture of Dulce de leche is the cherry on the top of these yummy mini cakes. Try it and we are sure you will become a fan if you are a sweet tooth and want to try something different.

Serving size: 10

Cooking time: 2 hours

Ingredients:

- White sugar ¾ cup
- Large egg 1
- All-purpose flour 1 cup
- Salt ¼ teaspoon
- Baking soda ½ teaspoon
- Baking powder 1 teaspoon
- Vanilla extract 1 ¼ teaspoons
- Softened unsalted butter ½ cup
- Milk ½ cup
- Frost Vanilla Marshmallow Fluffy Frosting ¾ lb.

For Dulce de Leche

- Sweetened condensed milk 1 0.9 lb. can
- Sea salt a large pinch

Instructions:

Preheat oven to around 350 F.

Use twelve paper liners to line the cupcake pan.

Beat the butter and sugar in a small bowl through the electric mixer. Keep beating until it becomes fluffy and light.

Add the vanilla extract and eggs into it and beat well.

Mix the salt, baking soda, and baking powder and beat well. Then add milk and flour while stirring well. Combine well.

Put the batter into the pan cups.

Bake the batter in the oven for 18 minutes and until they become light brown in color.

Let the cakes cool in the pan for at least 10 minutes.

To make Dulce de Leche, pour the condensed milk in a flat pan. Sprinkle salt and then cover it with a foil.

Place the pan in a larger pan and place it on the oven rack. Fill the larger pan using water halfway up.

Let it cook for 1 ½ hour and until the milk gets a good caramel color.

Remove the pan from the water bath and remove the foil. Whisk it until smooth and allow it to cool.

Fill every cupcake with dulce de leche 2 teaspoons. Pipe marshmallow frosting to cover it completely and enjoy.

Gale Boetticher's Vegan S'mores

Do you remember that German-American chemist who was working with Fring to create the drugs? One of the most important characters from this popular series, Gale Boetticher, is our inspiration behind this quick and easy recipe. Being single, it won't be easy for him to go for some extra fancy desserts. So, this extremely easy and quick recipe is the best pick for him and for all the fans who love sweets but can't manage time.

Serving size: 2

Cooking time: 5 minutes

Ingredients:

- Graham crackers 8
- Dark chocolate bar 1 (cut into four sections)
- Vegan marshmallows 4

Instructions:

Place the graham cracker upside down on the plate and add a chocolate chunk on the top.

Place marshmallow on its top and leave the top graham cracker on it.

When the marshmallow swells a lot, turn off the microwave.

Press this marshmallow down a little and add the second graham cracker on its top and voila! You are good to dig.

Classic Tres Leches Cake

We intentionally kept this recipe to conclude our cookbook because it deserved to be the showstopper in the book and on your table. If you have been reluctant to try this Tres Leches cake before due to the complexity of the recipes, you must be happy to read our recipe. Our very skilled experts have simplified it for you to try anytime you like.

Serving size: 20

Cooking time: 50 minutes

Ingredients:

- Yellow cake mix or butter recipe golden cake 1 package of regular size
- 3 Large eggs at room temperature
- 2% milk 2/3 cup
- Softened butter 1/2 cup
- Vanilla extract 1 teaspoon

For topping

- Sweetened condensed milk 1 can of 0.9 lb.
- Evaporated milk 1 can of 3/4 lb.
- Heavy whipping cream 1 cup

For whipped cream

- Heavy whipping cream 1 cup
- Confectioners' sugar 3 tablespoons
- Vanilla extract 1 teaspoon

Instructions:

Preheat the oven to about 350 F and grease a baking pan of 13x9-in.

Combine vanilla, softened butter, milk, eggs, and cake mix in a bowl and beat for about 30 seconds on low heat. Then beat on medium speed for 2 minutes.

Transfer it to the greased pan and bake for 30 to 35 minutes and cool on the wire rack for about 20 minutes.

Whisk the topping ingredients in a measuring cup until blended and poke holes in the warm cake's top using a skewer.

Pour the milk mixture over the cake slowly filling the holes and cool for 30 more minutes.

Refrigerate it covered for four hours or maybe overnight.

Beat the cream in a bowl until thickened.

Add vanilla and confectioners' sugar and beat it until the soft peaks are formed.

Spread it over the cake and enjoy.

Conclusion

Our super-talented team has left no stone unturned to collect the best recipes for the fans of Breaking Bad. The inspiration behind this book was not only the abundance of food scenes but the rich Mexican cuisine, which was the native place of the protagonists in this blockbuster series.

This cookbook is a beautiful collection of many recipes ranging from oh-so-common to super-luxury recipes containing seafood and other luxury ingredients. There are snacks that you can use for Breaking Bad watch parties and the entire variety of the main course dishes help you fix a wonderful menu for Breaking Bad themed parties.

About the Author

Contemporary Caribbean cuisine had never tasted so good before Rene Reed came into the scene. With about twenty years dedicated to building up a budding culinary career, Rene has worked in various top-end restaurants, hotels, and resorts as the head chef. Her dive into the food industry started in Michigan, where she trained with some of the best chefs on the block. Rene was an accountant at a top firm but didn't feel a sense of accomplishment at the end of the day. Something was missing, and although Rene didn't know it at that time, the answer was right under her nose.

She discovered how relaxed and happy she felt when she was trying to whip up something in the kitchen for her family. To her, cooking was equivalent to vacation time, where she could do whatever she wanted. Encouraged by her family and loved ones, Rene quit her job and started her culinary training in earnest. Her efforts yielded so much success as she built up a network that propelled her to key positions all around the industry.

She specializes in exceptional Caribbean cuisine while also adding that unique Rene touch to every menu as much as she can.

Author's Afterthoughts

Thank you for taking out time to read my work. I put in all those hours, and I'm super glad that you found it worthy enough to download. I would love to ask for one more thing, and that is your feedback. It will be lovely to know your thoughts on the contents of the book. Was it worth your time? Would you like me to change anything for my subsequent books? I'll love to hear them all.

Thanks!

Rene Reed

Lightning Source UK Ltd.
Milton Keynes UK
UKHW031820190223
417247UK00008B/875